MANAGERS IN DISGUISE-LEADERS IN DISGUST

THE NOT-SO OBVIOUS ROADBLOCKS TO SUCCESS

Robert E. Wood

authorHOUSE®

AuthorHouse™
1663 Liberty Drive
Bloomington, IN 47403
www.authorhouse.com
Phone: 1 (800) 839-8640

Published by AuthorHouse 12/16/2016

ISBN: 978-1-5246-0791-3 (sc)
ISBN: 978-1-5246-0789-0 (hc)
ISBN: 978-1-5246-0790-6 (e)

Library of Congress Control Number: 2016907634

Print information available on the last page.

Foreword

Are you fulfilled in your career? If so, you'll recognize many of the principles in this book as already being part of your business culture. If not, this book will expose something in need of a tweak. In either case, something can stand to be improved. Everyone, and I mean everyone, can have—and should have—successful, fulfilling careers.

As in anything, careers have peaks and valleys where periods of fulfillment and even prosperity wax and wane. That's a given. In the many years I've known Robert Wood, I've witnessed him not only enjoy the peaks but also rise above the valleys of his career path. He holds steady in whatever challenges because he knows it's not all about him. In whatever he does (as you'll see in this book), he recognizes that the greatest return on his own personal investments of time, effort, and care comes from the good, competent, passionate people that surround him, so he invests in their collective needs before his own. He's got their backs, so to speak, and in turn, they have his. When a competent person puts extra emphasis on caring for and elevating others and encourages others to elevate one another all toward a common goal, everything any professional would want rises—attendance, credibility, efficiency, functionality, fulfillment, morale, profits, satisfaction, and so on. The possibilities are endless.

I'm so glad Robert decided to write down these thoughts, and I think you'll appreciate them as much as I do. Let them soak in, apply them, commit to them, and watch in amazement as good things happen.

—Andy Moore

Acknowledgments

Special thanks to my loving wife, Claudia, and my two sons, Brandon and Justin, who have always pushed me to do better. I thank them for being patient with me during the time it took to put my thoughts on this paper.

I must give thanks to my friend and fellow author John R. Grubbs, best-selling author of *Leadership among Idiots* and *Leading the Lazy*. In 2005 he was instrumental in getting me started down the leadership path, and for that, I am forever grateful.

Thanks to my friend Floyd Rumbaugh, the driving force behind my actually sitting down and finally putting my words to paper. I took to him very quickly. He was one of my college instructors and offered more knowledge than he had to for a stranger. Floyd is a writer himself, writing stories and poetry.

Thanks to my nephew Jeff Clark of jeffclarkdesign.tv. He is an Emmy-nominated and Gold Broadcast Design Award–winning art director with a BS in media arts and animation. He is also the one responsible for the book's amazing cover. Thanks, Jeff.

Robert E. Wood

Finally I will thank my friends who were instrumental in making my work become reality: Andy Moore, Cullen Parks, Dewana Dorsey, Larry Richardson, Leigh Ann Richmond, and Scott Anson. They each have taken time out of their working lives to assist me with my work while asking nothing in return. Thank you all once again.

Table of Contents

1. My Personal View 1

2. The Heart of the Matter 5

3. Leadership Qualities 13

4. Our Teams 17

5. The Finer Details 23

6. Choices and Opportunities 29

7. It's a Two-Way Street 33

8. Dots to Connect for Success 41

9. Spreading the Love 47

10. Incentives = Retention 53

11. Performance and Seniority 57

12. Set Up to Fail 59

13. The Transition 65

14. Steps to Success 69

15. Overcoming the Roadblocks to Success 71

16. Terminations 77

17. Hiring 83

Introduction

This book is not another leadership how-to. Judging by the apparent shortage of effective leadership in our world today, one could conclude that so-called leaders don't comprehend how-to books. So in my journey to help organizations become more successful, I have found myself on the road less traveled. The timeless struggles between the qualified and the unqualified have led me to write about *positions of authority* and how to get the most out of them, instead of how to get the most out of the people in them.

My intention in writing this book is to relay the experiences and the insight I have gained over my thirty years in several different industries as well as disseminate practical success principles in a mature, commonsense way. I hope to improve the working lives of everyone by making the complicated not so complicated. I'm not writing about how to build a utopian environment or achieve perfection. I am writing about how we can and should always strive for perfection, even while knowing it is unattainable.

My intention is also to highlight the differences between managers in disguise and true leaders and to expose the not-so-obvious habits and deceptive tactics that managers in disguise commonly use. People are who they are; they either possess the skills necessary to lead, or they don't. The real question here is, how can we get willing leaders into the positions of authority that are occupied by unwilling managers? The answer to this question is dependent on the given organizational culture. An organizational culture is usually driven by an executive or a group of executives. All who care to make a difference must first ask, is the executive or group at the top of the organizational chart a member of the willing or the unwilling? If the top executives are members of the unwilling, then they are where you must start. You must find a way to get a member of the willing at the top, and then you will find it easier to get more of the willing into positions of authority.

There are willing leaders all around us who have been taught how to lead in some way, shape, or form. Some of them are hiding in plain sight, just waiting for the right bus to come along so they can do their work without feeling as if they're wasting their time. The right bus might be in the form of new leadership or a transfer to a different area within the organization. People know when they've found their calling; they become happier and more inspired. People's desire to be inspired is strong, so why not inspire? It's my belief that the organizations that put values before profits have the most profits due to their inspiring cultures. We must seek out these willing leaders, make sure they're in the right seats, and then get out of their way so they can do the work of inspiring others.

So if you've found yourself dealing with these same types of questions and issues and feel that the willing aren't being given their fair shot, this book is for you. Thank you and enjoy.

Chapter 1

<u>My Personal View</u>

My father is a navy vet, former long-haul truck driver, and very simple man. I'm the way I am because of him. He showed me that simply meeting expectations isn't enough; that's all most people do, and it's impossible to set yourself apart by doing what most people do. Because of my father, attempting to exceed expectations is all I know. I have found that living life as a highly proactive person by continually striving to exceed expectations reaps great rewards. I'm not a man of great means, but I am passionate about making things as great as possible. I try to exceed expectations all day, every day. I pay close attention to the responses of the people I'm trying to inspire. Through their actions and responses to my approach, I am able to determine how I'm doing. My hope is to be remembered one day as a man that everyone knew they could count on: the dependable, resourceful man that the people around me always wanted.

The difficult we do immediately. The
impossible takes a little longer.

—Motto of the US Army Corps of
Engineers during World War II

I'm a military man. I joined the army when I was eighteen, right out of high school. Over the years I've held many positions: managing partner, shop foreman, supervisor, trainer, mechanic, electrician, plumber, electronics tech, and nondestructive testing technician. Through all these careers, I've stayed bent on being a lifelong team player.

To quote the great Hunter Phillips, my close friend and neighbor, "It's good to learn from your mistakes; it's better to learn from someone else's." I focus on this all the time, which means I'm not wasting my time on history repeating itself. I don't want to sound as if I only see bad things happening. I do see and appreciate good things, but at times when I look around, I wonder if I'm the only one who sees that something bad is about to happen or in the process of happening. Furthermore, sometimes I wonder if I'm the only guy around who sees how to go about correcting the factors that led to the bad situation so it doesn't happen again. Notice I said *sometimes*—I'm not claiming to be an oracle. I believe those of us who are as proactive and passionate about doing great things in life tend to see the finer details more easily and more often because our vision is focused on greatness.

Take, for instance, the difference between substandard and great leadership. It has become apparent to me that most organizations do not know there is a difference. When it comes to positions of authority, most organizations believe that the authority alone is all that's needed to make a great leader, so they stick to promoting or hiring whoever is willing, even if the willing aren't capable. Not everyone has to be a great leader, but there must always be effective leaders in positions of authority because most managers don't possess the ability to open the full power and potential of their teams, while true leaders will have their teams charging hell with buckets of water while making it look easy. An effective leader is more likely to recognize change in the normal state of affairs and address potentially adverse issues before the negative effects get out of acceptable limits. A leader will also tend to be cognizant of the direction the organization is headed and better prepared to properly navigate the impending roadblocks. Last but not least, leaders recognize their own weaknesses and surround themselves with talented people who can do what the leaders cannot do themselves. This is what customers and teammates want and expect. This is inspiring. The following chart summarizes the differences between leaders and managers in disguise.

Leaders	Managers in Disguise
• earn respect	• earn contempt
• motivate	• discourage
• create more leaders	• create followers
• hold themselves accountable	• blame others
• give	• take
• are proactive	• are reactive
• communicate openly	• are secretive
• say *we*	• say *I*
• are disciplined	• are undisciplined
• inspire	• command
• are people focused	• are work focused
• are inclusive	• exclude
• are disciplined	• are reckless

Chapter 2

The Heart of the Matter

One could deduce from the name of this book that I hold anyone above me in contempt. I assure you this is not the case. In today's lean culture, we're doing all we can do to make the process work for us instead of working for the process, like modifying and organizing assembly lines so fewer people are needed to operate them or cutting out waste in day-to-day office operations to reduce staff. This is great stuff as long as we're not selfish about it. I believe in streamlining everything from politics to manufacturing. But when organizations begin combining a lot of jobs into one for the sake of efficiency and profits, they should stop when they get to the supervisory and executive leadership positions that steer the organization and influence large groups of employees.

The indirect cost of combining leadership roles with other time-consuming duties—like filling in on a production line for extended periods of time, collecting hourly inventory and production data, or running errands for the boss—is massive. This mesh of duties is a huge problem for the government and private blue-collar and white-collar organizations. This approach does not add value and is not cost effective. I also understand the pressures involved in trying to do two jobs at the same time. I've tried it myself and found it to be inefficient. My job as a leader was to build more leaders and be a resource for the teams. Then one day my manager decided that I could be more beneficial to the company if I worked on a few weeklong projects while performing my normal duties. The teams didn't care much for the idea. They felt as if their resources were gone and we were neglecting them by not investing as much time in training them up to be our replacements. Motivation went down, and so did production. I worked very hard to exceed everyone's expectations, but the costs stemming from poor morale, poor production, and a downward-trending on-time delivery rate were just too high. Instead of doing one thing well, I was doing two things poorly, and this was unacceptable for me, the team, and our customers.

Many organizations, both government and private, combine jobs and then refuse to address problems that arise. They may be choosing to keep things the way they are for the following reasons:

1. They have made quid pro quo and pay-to-play deals with lobbyists, constituents, and/or their employees that have to be fulfilled.

2. They refuse to admit to making a bad decision.

3. They think the problem is too difficult to fix.

4. They won't demote or discipline their buddies.

What happened to continuous improvement? When private-sector organizations or politicians put lobbyists or profits before their constituents' or employees' expectations, valuable power and potential are lost. Here is the solution: separate the leadership role from any and every other duty. This is a win-win for everyone. Put values before profits, proactively invest in your people, and stop making sophomoric decisions. Then you will find your charts and graphs headed in the right direction. This makes business sense. When changes need to be made, real leaders don't hesitate. They act swiftly because it's what they are expected to do. But beyond that, it's the right thing to do—the moral thing to do—because the leader's main goal should be to keep all the teams moving forward as best they can. The teams expect greatness on every level. Lead by example, meet as many expectations as is reasonably possible, don't hesitate to do what's right, and be an actual resource to your teammates. Soon, you'll be a leader in your own right.

Another difference between a manager in disguise and a true leader is the manager in disguise always thinks everything will be all right and so feels no sense of urgency, while the leader believes the bottom is about to fall out and is always thinking about how he or she can prevent it. A manager in disguise will typically have a reactive mentality, while a leader will always have a proactive mentality. For instance, a manager in disguise will not voluntarily invest time or money in training his or her employees. He or she would rather wait and react to the needs of the customers instead of being proactive and getting out in front of the markets. With this reactive mentality, the odds of not being able to meet the customers' expectations in a timely manner increase dramatically.

I have experienced on numerous occasions people's ability and willingness to be a drag on an entire neighborhood, company, city, state, or even country strictly for selfish reasons. Have you heard the saying "One bad apple can ruin the whole bunch"? Of course you have! I once worked in an organization that used seniority as the basis for its employee-retention program. Once the worst employees of the organization, the type of people I call C team members, accrued enough seniority, they really began to take advantage of the system (the different teams that make up organizations will be more thoroughly discussed later on, in chapter 4). No matter how bad their attendance or production was, their seniority kept them safe. The C team's lack of respect for their work, teammates, and attendance was discouraging to everyone, but there was nothing their teammates could do about it. The C team selfishly delivered the bare minimum needed to keep their jobs. This is exactly what I'm writing about. Too many good, hardworking people have been negatively affected in all sorts of ways by a bad apple in the bunch. Other people's arrogance, dishonesty, and sophomoric decision-making abilities have hurt them. This is unfortunate and unnecessary.

Leadership is not for everyone, because there is no easy way out for a leader. For a true leader, there is no lobbyist influencing decisions, no hiding place, and no carpet to sweep things under. A true leader would rather disappoint you with the truth than make you happy with a lie. Leaders approach every issue with a sense of urgency because they know their teams gave them the power and the trust they have for this very reason. When the goal is greatness, managers in disguise will stand out like sore thumbs. Should they be allowed to keep riding along and dragging everything and everyone else down with them, including the people who put them there? No. Note that I refer to them as *managers in disguise* because a leader wouldn't allow the team or the culture to suffer unnecessarily. A leader doesn't tolerate uncooperative behavior; therefore, a culture of corruption is less likely to exist. Every day, true leaders will ask, "Did I do everything I could do today to make this place great?" On the other hand, managers in disguise, knowing they are in over their heads, will ask, "How can I play with my words and the data to make myself look good?" Failing managers should be reevaluated to determine whether or not they should be sent back to their former positions. A leader knows that once a problem is found, it must immediately be properly addressed— even removed if necessary. A problem employee must never be promoted beyond his or her ability or level of competence.

A manager in disguise is a manager in a position of authority who has no apparent leadership skills and knows it. It is a manager who lives in fear of losing his or her position yet refuses to step aside for the greater good of all affected. He or she may have a foul mouth and a nobody-ever-measures-up-to-my-standards attitude. You know them, the ones everyone, including the paying customers, complains about. Or they might be frat-boy types who believe their affiliations are more important than their accomplishments. True leaders can align the team's interests with the organization's interests and vice versa. If only true leaders are allowed to be in positions of authority, then the interests of everyone involved have a greater chance of aligning and adding value to the system with each step forward.

Everyone wants to work for an organization they feel is headed in the right direction. Everyone wants to be a part of something bigger. Everyone wants their opinions heard and understood. No one wants the quality of their efforts swept under the carpet while being forced to sit by and watch as some manager in disguise gets or takes credit for the quality of others' efforts. A true leader can achieve great things by not caring about who gets the credit, but not everyone is or wants to be a true leader. For instance, those who do not want the responsibility that comes with authority but still put forth a quality effort every hour on the job still need the quality of their efforts noticed for their own personal reasons.

Managers in disguise are the most expensive and ineffective people on the payroll. Take into account the people who put them there and their willingness to keep them there. Though I have been able to connect these dots, I cannot understand why they are allowed to exist. If you've been in business for any amount of time, you've probably witnessed the many different steps to an extensive cover-up. You probably also understand that covering something up can be more difficult, expensive, and time consuming than just doing it right the first time. Doing it right the first time adds value. The benefits to doing everything right the first time rather than covering it up are huge. Here are just a few of the benefits:

- Morale goes up.

- Organizational Volunteer Percentage Rate grows.

- Profits rise.

- Waste goes down.

- Safety improves.

- Teams form.

I just can't understand why anyone would deliberately run any type of organization off the cliff for a quick buck. Unfortunately, a lack of leadership of this magnitude is readily available in most organizations at all levels. The lack of love, honor, integrity, and respect for others is destroying our ability to excel in the world. In most cases, you do not have to look far to find a leader in disgust to whom you should give an opportunity and a chance to make a difference. A leader in disgust is a member of your A team who is ready for the chance to lead formally and is truly disgusted by the amount of dysfunction the executive members of the C team are willing to put up with. A leader in disgust is ready, willing, and able to step up and do the leadership work that needs to be done. It's the politics of change that gets in the way of progress, creativity, productivity, and so on. After all, the organizations with the best employees are usually the ones who tactfully separate themselves from their competition through innovation, profits, and teamwork.

I take leadership very seriously. It's not a word to be taken lightly. It really bothers all those who aspire to be great leaders, such as myself, when we try our best to take three steps forward just to have some politician, executive, or manager in disguise take us two steps backward. This is all too common because these people lack the passion, proactivity, and/or desire it takes to earn the right to hold their positions. Everyone needs traction and a grip on things; nobody wants to be spinning his or her wheels without making progress.

Not everyone's quality effort is the same. The key is that it be *your* quality effort, not anyone else's. That is all anyone can and should expect of themselves or others. It is those who choose not to put forth their quality efforts that are the problem. There's a big difference between a plain effort and a quality effort. A plain effort is just enough to keep your job. A quality effort requires you to be the person you said you'd be when you interviewed for the job. Do you remember that person? When you were interviewed, in some form or fashion you were basically asked, "Why do I need your services over the other potential hires'?" You likely answered with something every employer wants to hear. It was probably something sharp like "I will put forth a quality effort for every hour on the job" or "I'm a highly proactive team player, and I will show up early and leave late." In the workplace, to gain influence, we must always strive to be that person we said we would be prior to our employment.

Chapter 3

<u>Leadership Qualities</u>

Nobody is perfect, but there is something to be said about those who will not go down without striving to be viewed as a leader. People who are passionate about their work and ready, willing, and able to learn the rest should always be an executive's first choice. So how can we identify true leaders? True leaders set themselves apart with these qualities:

- humility—Just because you know you're awesome doesn't mean you have to tell everybody; just show them.

- caring—People don't care how much you know until they know how much you care.

- honesty—It's called the best policy for a reason.

- candidness (but also tactfulness)—Be open and forthright yet respectful. Why hold back?

- approachability—Be friendly. Others won't be honest with you if they cannot approach you.

- good communication skills—Know how to say what you need to say.

- ability to motivate others—You don't necessarily have to be a cheerleader; just don't be discouraging.

- proactive mind-set—If you know something needs to be done, don't wait to be told to do it.

- professionalism—There may be some solid amateurs, but they still can't touch professionals.

- interactive approach—Get out there among the team.

- intellectual accessibility—Don't be overly preoccupied. Your team needs you!

- being a good student—You can never be too smart to learn from someone else.

- team focus—There is a bigger picture than just yourself.

- drive to meet or exceed expectations—This is simply the right way to be.

- ability to hold others accountable—Holding others accountable will help them to grow to handle more responsibility in the future.

- ability to give credit and award others—It is important to give credit where it's due but only do so when the person has earned it.

- fairness—The workplace is no place to play favorites.

Those who possess these qualities are both trusting and trustworthy. When just one of these qualities is removed, trust and respect begin to disappear. When evaluating all commanding positions, it is crucial to verify the existence of these qualities through perception and performance-feedback surveys.

Chapter 4

<u>Our Teams</u>

In every organization there are those who create messes and those who clean them up. The employees in any organization can be classified into three groups: A team, B team, and C team, with the A team being the best employees and the C team being the worst. A, B, and C team members can be found in all levels of the organization, from the entry-level positions to the highest leadership levels in the organization.

The A team is full of highly proactive team players who willingly put forth a quality effort for every hour on the job. These are your leaders, role models, and go-to people. These are the ones who unfortunately spend too much time cleaning up the messes. They're also the ones you miss the most when they're on vacation. These are the ones who will lead by example even though they may not be receiving the full financial benefits of the position.

The B team is full of highly proactive team players who also put forth a quality effort for every hour on the job but somehow fall short of the A team. They could be new hires and simply need more training, or maybe they don't quite grasp the big picture and their role within it. Whatever the shortcoming, they're very close to being on the A team.

The C team consists of a small, fluctuating percentage of employees (temporary and permanent) who create and sustain the messes. These are the ones who are unrealistic in their expectations about what they should and shouldn't be allowed to get away with. They're the ones with no sense of awareness or commitment to organizational success. Although they do not represent the majority of employees, the C team requires the bulk of the resources and never-ending maintenance. Those on this team aren't necessarily bad people, though I've noticed that in the past several years C team members have grown to be more defiant, disrespectful, and undisciplined. This entitlement mentality (planned obsolescence) allows C team people to say just about anything to get a job. They put a street-smart spin on their qualifications and misinform leaders as to their work ethic and abilities. This behavior has led to unjustified negative perceptions of the leaders who are supposed to make sure that only the right people are on the bus. Regularly scheduled turnovers of C teammates are a requirement for personal and organizational success. Small businesses are the least likely to have the resources to subsidize the C team. The usual thought process is that hiring a very well-qualified person is too expensive and that money can be saved by hiring an amateur instead. I've got news for you: that amateur will end up costing you ten times more than you ever expected.

The majority of the resources (personal and financial) that it takes to support all these teams is more often than not directed toward the C team. This is due to a whole host of issues stemming from allowing the C team to be on the bus in the first place. Yes, all three teams do share some of the same resources, but the A and B teams use the resources to add value, whereas the C team is more prone to waste these resources. In addition to wasting shared resources, C team members drain an unequally high proportion of the organization's resources because of issues like

- tardiness, which leads to disruptions in the flow of information, production, morale, and teamwork;

- lack of passion for their work, which leads to a lack of productivity, creativity, teamwork, morale, and quality; and

- disciplinary issues, which lead to disruptions in other departments, such as human resources, quality, and finance.

All these issues are *indirect costs*. The resources necessary to continually address these issues are very costly not only to the organization but to the members of the organization and their health and well-being. If these issues go unnoticed or, more importantly, are noticed and allowed to go uncorrected, they will sap the motivation right out of people in spite of their best efforts to keep a positive outlook.

I once worked for a company who had A and B team members led by members of the C team. This went on for a while because the executives always hired like-minded people. It just goes to show that a position at the top of the organizational chart doesn't automatically make one passionate about his or her work. This goes for politicians, executives, managers, employees, and so on. C team members are unable to muster passion for their jobs and are unwilling to correct this situation on their own. However, a great leader recognizes this lack of passion and does for C team members what they refuse to do for themselves: he or she sends them on their way with instructions to find work they are truly passionate about. A leader does not move C team members around from one position to another or one department to another, leaving a trail of disruption in their wake that is sure to stifle motivation. A leader uses situations like these as an opportunity to show the A and B teams that he or she knows and understands their expectations and makes their teams a priority.

True leaders don't knowingly let people who are miserable at their jobs continue to come to work. For one, it's unhealthy for the employee, and secondly, it puts an unnecessary burden on the rest of the teams. Consider the A and B teams, who day after day are forced to pull the C team's weight because some executive or manager thinks resolving this situation is not a top priority. Here's some insight for you: when you notice (whether through data analysis or by personal interaction) that A and B team members are hiding their power and potential in an attempt to force management's hand to fix a C team problem, then you've stumbled upon a massive managerial cover-up, and it's likely that all your charts and graphs are headed in the wrong direction. Such an issue is usually due to the C team's complacency and arrogance and due to C team members in leadership roles not sharing the whole truth (and nothing but the truth) in executive and managerial meetings.

When one person—just one person—continually plays with his or her words or manipulates the data, it undermines the integrity of every other piece of data you're acquiring. Think back to some news-making scandal that was exposed in a government office. Did the legitimacy of everything concerning that office immediately fall short in your mind? Once an item makes the news as being falsified from company so-and-so, suddenly everything about that company comes into question. One person should not be allowed to inflict this kind of damage on any organization.

Chapter 5

<u>The Finer Details</u>

Everyone wants the quality of their efforts to be recognized. There are three different ways people view the incentives offered to them:

1. They're not getting what they're worth.

2. They're getting fair incentives.

3. They're getting more than they deserve.

Employees who get promoted into authority positions usually adjust their lifestyles to match whatever compensation comes with those new positions. So such promotions should not be taken lightly; these decisions should be well thought out to not set anyone up for embarrassment or failure. This is one reason why it's so difficult to reverse a flippant or hasty promotion and demote someone when that ill-advised promotion doesn't turn out to be a successful one.

Managers in disguise who know they're not in the right seat on the bus will do just about anything to keep their prestigious positions and lifestyles. When they are faced with the thought of losing that lifestyle and are pressured to produce quality results, managers in disguise will be driven to make choices they normally wouldn't make, such as setting their teams up for failure to make themselves appear to be the only ones competent enough to do their jobs or fabricating stories about their activities to make themselves seem more valuable. Their refusal to step down is driven by selfishness and pride. Just the embarrassment of a demotion is enough to make some people take measures into their own hands in a desperate attempt to prolong or completely avoid the inevitable. Waiting to solve this problem only makes it worse for everyone.

Solution #1: Clarify goals, expectations, and dos and don'ts prior to promotion.

Too many people suddenly become different people after getting promotions that give them a little authority. This change is due to the fact that the goals and expectations associated with their new positions weren't thoroughly explained prior to them receiving their promotions. If you want your words to work magic, explain the dos and don'ts of the new position until there is nothing left open for the employee to interpret *prior* to offering him or her that position. Everyone should be held accountable from the moment they take their positions. This will reduce the frequency and magnitude of behavioral shifts from all affected by the position. Consistency in this regard is necessary. A disruption in productivity of any sort is automatically a loss in profits. When every person works where he or she is most qualified, the overall efficiency of the organization is greater.

Solution #2: Establish a probationary period.

The issue of people changing their lifestyles after getting a promotion can be avoided by withholding the new incentives until the recommended probationary period has expired and all the feedback has been collected and reviewed. Probationary periods should be mandatory for every promotion and new hire to allow for the gathering of appropriate, intelligent, and meaningful feedback. Once you receive the adequate and acceptable feedback from all affected, only then should a decision be made whether or not another change is in order. Failure to accept the team's feedback and advice means that from then on the team will make sure you get credit for your own poor decision making.

Solution #3: Have the leader ask the teams, "How am I doing?"

There is a big difference between an employee's behavior and effort, yet they are directly connected. When someone's behavior makes a transition from good to bad, his or her effort usually declines as well out of spite. When this happens, not only does the team member suffer, but everyone else does too. Conversely, when behavior transitions from bad to good, effort builds. A team's behaviors and corresponding efforts fluctuate depending on how the team members feel at any given time. This is why fair and consistent discipline is crucial for stability. It's not the policies, programs, and procedures that are responsible for this fluctuation in behavior and effort; it's the lack of proactively monitoring the implementation and enforcing of those policies, programs, and procedures. If you say you're going to do something, then do it! A lot of the issues organizations have (policy violations, tardiness, poor quality, lack of teamwork, and so on) are directly related to the organization's culture. Lack of sincere, caring, compassionate leadership and failure to deliver on the team's expectations of management is a surefire way to diminish morale.

For those managers who feel their teams have marginalized them and their position due to lack of results and inaction, I have good news. All the information you need to change your team's perception of you is readily available. All you need to do is ask the teams, "What do you expect out of me?" and listen to the answer. Then deliver on those expectations, request performance feedback on your progress, and repeat the cycle every day, all day. I have found that if you look around, you'll find members of the A team actually leading management by example. Remember, the A team members are true leaders. They try to show management how to achieve quality results by using the bottom-up style of leadership. The members of the A team are committed to success and believe that someone has to lead by example, and if you're not going to do it, they might as well take action. Their goal is for their style to inspire everyone around to achieve the most they can. Everyone should watch the A team for a bit to see how it's done. If you believe this approach to be beneath an office of leadership, you might be a manager in disguise. There is no room for this mentality in true leadership. You should reconsider your thoughts because, in reality, expectations are a two-way street.

One might think that the managers-in-disguise approach to leadership, combined with the voluntary subsidization of the C teams, would be enough to inspire someone to take a look at the charts and graphs, call a meeting, and make some changes, but that would require a true leader to be in a position of authority.

Managers in disguise don't worry about their image; they believe it can only be good because of their positions. This is why they appear to not care about what the team needs or wants. They feel they can make decisions as they see fit without repercussions. Image doesn't come with the position, though. Through a manager's actions, the team will perceive that manager's true image, regardless of what that manager believes his or her image to be.

Chapter 6

<u>Choices and Opportunities</u>

For those wannabe great leaders of the world who are fed up with substandard leadership styles and techniques, there are great opportunities for you. Each person has the right to step up to the plate and lead by example. You can choose to take action and lead if you want to. Your chain of command may have something to say about this move, though. Depending on your organization's culture, their response to your actions could be one of praise or dissatisfaction. The managers in disguise may put pressure on you to stop you from being recognized as the team's true leader instead of them. If this happens and your intentions are purely to make a positive difference, you should remind them that you are only being the person you said you were going to be *when they hired you*—that is, a highly proactive team player who will put forth a quality effort every hour on the job. It's hard to argue with that stance. Of course we all hope the quality of our efforts is recognized and celebrated in a professional manner. However, sometimes through our actions, we leave too much to interpretation, and this creates questions about our motives instead of friendly competition between teammates. Although actions speak louder than words, to avoid leaving too much to interpretation, we should use our words in conjunction with our actions to make sure there's no mistaking exactly what our intentions are. Managers in disguise who see up-and-coming teammates might feel threatened and typically will assume the teammates are after their jobs or out to make them look bad. Of course it's all about them, so the managers in disguise can't admit that these up-and-comers are doing a great job, taking ownership of the situation, separating themselves from their competition, and earning the right to have better seats on the bus. Those teammates are actually being the people they said they were going to be when they were hired over all those other potential hires.

Common sense isn't so common. The up-and-coming teammates should just keep doing their best with consistent discipline. They are simply doing what they know is right and defining themselves as true leaders. Through the quality of their efforts, they should get promotions—because the team wants it and demands it. Remember, it's not the position and title that define a person as a leader; those things just allow a leader to influence more people and have more time to spend on passionate leadership pursuits (exceeding expectations).

Managers in disguise who choose to not improve their situations do so for selfish reasons. Their teams expect and deserve better. What gets my blood boiling are the managers who get constructive feedback from team members and squander the opportunity to add value to the process, which could add value to everything else in turn. Why would they waste these opportunities? Let's consider some of the reasons:

- The solution wasn't their idea, and they either don't want to credit others or cannot find a way to take the credit for themselves.

- Implementing the solution would involve too much work or might force them to actually do their job.

- He or she may have to move a buddy into a different seat or off the bus altogether to make things right.

For ultimate success, you must have managers in management positions and leaders in every level of your organization. That may sound farfetched, but people will show their true leadership potential if they're in the right seat on the bus, in the right environment with the right encouragement. Let me stress that everyone absolutely *must* be in the right seat on the bus. This means people should be placed in positions that complement their strengths. Proper placement will lead directly to improved morale, proactivity, creativity, safety, teamwork, and ultimately production. This is the solid foundation of a successful organization. If a right seat cannot be found for someone, he or she should be taken off the bus altogether in order for the team to have any hopes for success. Look around your situation. Are you on the right bus? Are you in the right seat on the bus? If not, you should ask yourself, "What does the team expect of me?" You need to be proactive and discuss which seat, if any, is right for you.

The goal of all wannabe great leaders is to make a difference and inspire others to do and be something to remember, not throw their teammates under the bus. Too often, managers in disguise have the perception that the aspiring leader's motives are to inflict some kind of pain on them in an attempt to make them look bad rather than recognizing that the aspiring leader is simply doing an exceptional job for the benefit of everyone. Often, managers in disguise and other members of the C team use these deceptive and deflective approaches (tactics used to make up for their shortcomings) to great success for themselves but to the detriment of everyone else in the organization.

If you are a manager in disguise, then you probably don't care much for the thought of a highly proactive team player getting hired or transferred into your department. This is when the real fun begins. Playtime is over; it's time to put up or shut up, time to put on an ethical display, roll up those sleeves, and start delivering on all those expectations you've been neglecting to exceed. We all have choices to make and opportunities to seize. If a typical side effect of a leader doing a great job means the manager or executive has to step up and retake control of the driver's seat, then so be it. If you choose not to step up, then you choose not to keep your job. There is nobody else to blame or point the finger at; the status quo is unacceptable.

Chapter 7

It's a Two-Way Street

When it comes to teammates, every teammate is a customer. Each teammate has expectations that need to be met in a timely manner. Even beyond teammates, each constituent or employee is your customer. If you give teammates what they need, when they need it, with superior quality, you will begin unlocking the power and potential of the entire team. This will jump-start the competitive edge you need to separate yourself and your organization from your competition.

The fact that some executives and managers refuse to see that expectations are a two-way street still bothers me. The holier-than-thou, arrogant attitudes of some politicians, executives, and managers while they hide in their offices with the need for nameplates on their doors and desks and personalized reserved parking spots are dead ends for any team. Corrupt politicians have the system rigged, executives are usually so high up the organizational chart that there is no one else for them to answer to, and as for the failing managers in disguise, well, they usually have the executives covering for them. This situation is unfortunate for the rest of the team; they will just have to wait out these managers in disguise and will more than likely withhold their potential until they see a positive change in direction from management. These arrogant types hold their positions for selfish reasons, all the while training up their assistants and replacements. Their calculation is that no one will recognize their shortcomings. These types shoot themselves in the foot all the time and usually don't realize it until it's too late, when all the damage has already been done. Their lack of leadership skills will show up on someone's radar ... eventually, but by the time it does, there will have already been losses in creativity and motivation, which is too bad. Everyone's motivation as well as their passion and willingness to follow what executives and managers have to say directly affects the bottom line. When you project weakness, your teams will respond accordingly.

Truly effective leaders do not need this type of vanity. A long title says nothing about their character and is unnecessary. They need their fingers on the pulse of their teams. They need to implement the 80-20 plan, where 80 percent of their time is dedicated to servant leadership (exceeding expectations) and 20 percent of their time is spent taking care of value-added office work. This approach genuinely inspires the organization 100 percent of the time. I'm not saying organizations don't need executives and managers. What I'm saying is that executives and managers can make decisions all day long and probably be great at it, but if they get too busy with their own office work to notice their workers are suffering due to lack of resources or other unfulfilled needs, then expectations will never fully be met. It's the true leaders who take the decisions handed down from executive management as they are and turn them into reality.

Oftentimes the people at the top are not of our choosing, and the team's opinions aren't even sought after. Too many times, managers in disguise will hire or promote people with no real potential, like their classmates, friends, relatives, or outsiders with good-looking résumés. Managers in disguise often don't even bother getting any idea of a person's character before hiring or promoting him or her. Been there, done that, got the T-shirt! A manager who aspires to be a true leader will ask himself or herself in this situation, "What does the team expect of me?" Then he or she will find the answer and deliver on those expectations. Arrogance is the quickest way to stop success. You can assume you are meeting or even exceeding expectations and probably be correct a little bit of the time, or you can be proactive and ask your teams and customers what their expectations are and be correct 99 percent of the time. The use of perception and performance-feedback surveys is a must. Stop assuming and get some real data, crunch those numbers, prioritize items, and start delivering.

Managers in disguise are in charge only as long as the team members allow them to be in charge. If you're a manager in disguise and think I'm wrong in this perception, ask yourself, "What is needed to be considered in charge, and do I have it?" This exercise, if performed honestly, will be an eye-opener. Once your team members don't want you as their boss because of any reason of their choosing, they will hide their potential, withhold their efforts, or just go somewhere else and find another boss. Then what do you have? When people hide their potential, goals suffer. If profits drop due to lack of productivity, morale, teamwork, creativity, safety, and/or respect, there is nothing you can do about it, as you are outnumbered—there are more teammates than there are you. Do you really think your disguise can shelter you from the trending data? When the charts and graphs start dropping for no apparent reason, someone will feel the need to investigate. If you have honestly been putting forth a quality effort to be successful as a leader but just do not have enough passion for your position, you will probably be asked to find another seat that is better suited for you. On the other hand, if you have been taking advantage of your position, your team, and the person or people who put you there, you should have your résumé ready because you will most likely be asked to seek other opportunities elsewhere. A strong community with proven results of self-management, safety, quality, and productivity can influence any organization's decision-making process.

Think about the companies who are somewhat successful in spite of themselves. They might not be able to get out of their own way until the C team members in executive positions retire or finally get noticed by those they answer to and get rotated out. These companies may be run like dictatorships, with the executives being masters and the employees being students. The managers in disguise in these organizations might refuse to let go and might fail to understand that the need to meet expectations is definitely a two-way street. We all answer to each other in some way. Companies have reasonable expectations of their employees, and employees have expectations of their companies. When everyone is focused on meeting each other's expectations, then you have the beginnings of a solid foundation to build on. If you are in a position of authority and lack the intestinal fortitude to put forth a quality effort for every minute of every hour of every day, then you are one of the roadblocks to success that is going to keep your entire organization from reaching its full potential.

If you have authority and suspect your subordinates have marginalized you and your position, your days may be numbered. Being marginalized means whatever you're doing or have already done is not being received in a favorable manner. Just because you are in a position of authority doesn't mean everything is just going to fall into place. It doesn't mean the team will want to socialize with you or even respect you. Organizations can and will promote who they want, when they want. This doesn't mean team members are going to respect these decisions. You still have to prove yourself. Making arrogant decisions and dismissing the team's expectations will almost certainly damage trust, which will take a long time to rebuild. The team's attitude will not change until you accept the fact that your way is not working. You're going to have to swallow your pride and ask the team, "What can I do to be a part of the solution?" The team's unfavorable attitude is not a form of disrespect; it's just no respect. If you choose to stay the course, you choose to struggle. It's not a mutiny; it's a team of adults who are working together for the greater good of the organization. You will have to listen to the team and deliver on their expectations if you want yourself and your position to be successful. No one is immune to the team members' ability to get their point across. Their desire to be successful far outweighs any one person's desire for the status quo. Like I said before, there are more of them than there are of you. Remember, just being a leader is not as important as who you become on your journey.

I've tried top-down and bottom-up leadership. Top down is by far the most effective as long as the person at the top is truly committed to putting values before profits. The bottom-up style of leadership will only get you so far, but you still have to hope your ability to lead by example and produce consistent results rubs off on the executives and managers in disguise as leaders. If great results do not come down from the top, a loving, passionate, and caring team of adults can try to send great results up from the bottom.

More often than not, organizations use social media as a tool to keep tabs on their employees. They will connect with as many employees as possible and then have some loyal office worker keep tabs on what's being said about the organization. This action, as long as the information gathered is looked at objectively and used constructively, can be a useful tool. I've known many people who have posted the good and bad about their organizations' issues. This information, when used correctly, can add value to any organization.

It's been my experience that when someone praises his or her organization, or a part of it, on a social media site, this information is dismissed as not worthy of discussion. On the other hand, when someone steps up and posts a comment that can be construed as negative, he or she is immediately hauled into an office and instructed to cease all negative posts about the organization. My issue with this is not the attempt to protect the organization's image but rather the lack of any attempt to address and resolve the issues that led to the negative post in the first place.

When employees or constituents offer positive or negative information about what's going on in their working lives, their insight should be taken seriously. The legitimacy of all claims should be verified. All too often, the goal is just to squash the negative publicity without ever addressing the problem. However, the goal should be to use the information to the organization's advantage. If you *truly* want the number of negative posts to decrease and the positive ones to increase, you must take the good with the bad. Ask the employees or constituents what their expectations are and how you can better serve them, and then deliver on those expectations. Failure to address the issue is a failure on your part to be a part of the solution. There's no value added in the collection of information if there is no effective plan to take action on that information.

Chapter 8

Dots to Connect for Success

An organization's successes and failures are directly related to the answers to these questions:

1. *Do profits come at the expense of values?*

Putting profits before values will give you short-term profits and long-term struggles. This approach is readily recognizable to even the newest teammate and doesn't garner any respect. True organizational success just isn't possible if your customers or your teams view you as not having any integrity or values.

2. *Are only the right people on the bus, and are they where they belong on the bus?*

To have monumental success, a company must first have the right people on the bus, and they all must be in the right seats. Success starts with a firm foundation and then solid layers added on. A firm foundation consists of only the right people on the bus. They are the ones who are passionate about what they're doing and capable of learning the rest.

3. Is the scheduled employee turnover rate of the C team enforced?

Once you've identified a person as a member of the C team, then he or she no longer really belongs on your bus.

4. Is information flowing freely, or is it abused and used as a way to hold power over the teams?

Information shouldn't be kept in the dark, by anyone. This creates a reactive instead of a proactive culture.

5. Are members of the C team allowed to train their replacements, conduct performance evaluations, or be involved in the hiring/firing process?

Someone who is clearly on the C team will be unable to train anyone far beyond his or her own level. He or she also will be unable to evaluate or properly staff what he or she cannot comprehend. Any C teammate who is allowed to perform these duties will only fluster and exasperate others.

6. Is the team's behavior and potential (safety, ethics, proactivity, creativity, and so on) affecting charts and graphs positively or negatively?

Production is directly influenced by the A and B teams' willingness to follow management's direction. If the A and B teams believe management is incompetent, they will do the bare minimum to keep their jobs until they see some positive change.

7. *Are managers in disguise constantly downplaying their teams' abilities to make themselves look like the only one capable of being in charge?*

The most effective type of leader will have employees that are capable of assuming his or her duties at a moment's notice. A manager in disguise attempts to stifle his or her employees' ability to do this.

8. *Is the organization counting on managers in disguise to actually increase profits?*

If so, the managers in disguise are likely actually draining profits. A loss of profits is the main risk associated with allowing managers in disguise to fill positions of authority.

9. *Are good employees quitting? If so, why?*

Good employees never look to leave organizations, but they will leave managers in disguise as leaders.

10. *Are valuable assets being directed toward the C team?*

If so, they are draining those resources and diverting them from other teams that could use them more effectively.

The basis of organizational success is the ability to continuously connect and address these points of interest consistently.

A company can implement all the great ideas and do all the calculations and still find itself struggling to achieve its latest goal. Nine times out of ten, the engineers' numbers and designs are well thought out, vetted, and worth a try, so the company implements their ideas and automatically has issues. Wow! There's a head-scratcher for you. Who saw this coming? When things don't go as expected, it's not always the fault of the person charged with continuous improvement of processes. Most of these people don't make changes just to say they did it; they're passionate about what they do and have a need to see their vision and solutions realized. When failures in continuous process improvements like this occur, it's usually because the overseers are crunching corrupt data they received from C team members.

For example, a Kaizen expert was charged with optimizing a production cell process with a goal of cranking out fifty whatchajiggles per hour. The expert studied the equipment and layout and determined that with a simple rearrangement of tasks the goal was easily attainable. So he implemented his changes and went on his way. Soon after, he received feedback that nothing was progressing as he'd assured everyone that it would before he left. The expert made his way back to the production cell to observe the new arrangement in operation. It didn't take him long to realize that the cell operators didn't like the new arrangement and had taken it upon themselves to put the cell back the way it had been prior to his involvement without telling anyone. From the floor employees all the way to the top executive, an effective team hadn't been built that would work together properly for the success of the company. They were determined to simply stay in their comfort zone and make the expert's ideas fail so they wouldn't have to embrace change.

This is what happens when members of the C team are allowed to promote or train their like-minded replacements. This is what I mean when I say people should not be promoted to their level of incompetence. Know this: most people live beyond their means, so they welcome promotions past their levels of competence. They think these promotions will help them live within their means, but really the promotions only make it worse. This type of promotion is not only bad for the promoted but also for everyone else in the entire organization. Once someone has been promoted with a pay increase, there's no stepping down, no going back, and the promoted person's lack of solid results is realized by everyone. Waiting to solve this flippant promotion only makes it worse. Picture, for instance, the problems associated with the extra time, extra personnel, and extra resources it takes to support incompetence. Supporting incompetence is very taxing on all teammates in the organization. Organizations would do themselves a great bit of good if the executives and managers would ask each other just two questions: What was the requirement? and What did you do? This is accountability at its best. Make the requirements known and clear, leave nothing to interpretation, and hold people accountable with consistent discipline.

Organizational success depends on whether or not you put the cart before the horse. Profits will be proportional to the team's passion for their work. To be the lowest-cost provider with the highest quality and on-time delivery rate, the team must always come first. An organization's ability to separate itself from its competition is just as much a credit to the team as it is the leadership's decision-making process. The customer is surely the final judge and jury on the matter. So I do not recommend you run your part of an organization as if you are the only one in charge, because you're not.

Chapter 9

<u>Spreading the Love</u>

In a perfect world, we wouldn't have to ask for someone to look out for our best interests in the same manner as we look out for theirs just to make sure the quality of our efforts doesn't go unnoticed. This world isn't perfect. Believe it or not, there are people on the wrong bus. There are people who will take credit for what you and your team have done, people who will hold you back to make themselves look better, and people who will withhold critical information from you so they can use it against you later. It's because the world isn't perfect that we all must stand up and praise those who have earned the right to be praised and expose the weaknesses of those who have earned the right to be exposed. The easiest way to do that is to earn the right seat on the bus and take actions to purposefully inspire your teammates to look out for you as you do them. There is power and safety in numbers. I believe we should be impartial to everyone in our care—including the C team members, even though they aren't as passionate about their work as they need to be—right up until the time they decide to move on or get moved on. We should freely offer everyone respect, honesty, and a sincere commitment to their general health and well-being. This act of kindness fosters a healthy environment, which leads to a culture of real teamwork and success.

Think about the unemployed potential hires that are actually passionate about your organization and the potential it has to offer. Imagine a downturn in the economy and the struggles the unemployed go through due to no fault of their own. Now imagine receiving a letter such as this one from one of those unemployed (letter written by keynote speaker and best-selling author John Grubbs):

> Dear Hiring Manager,
>
> I am confused about your frequent complaints regarding the availability of talented people for your organization. You complain that good workers are difficult to find. Help me understand your position and perspective because I just cannot understand your logic.
>
> Currently, there are people on your team who do not perform, do not show up, and do not appreciate the job they are asked to complete. Yet you cannot seem to find the desire or ability to remove them from your team. What gives?
>
> There are many of us who will very much appreciate that job. We will be there on time (even early). We will give you everything we have, and

we will even help you find others like us. Do you not know we are out here?

We cannot understand why you allow those people who speak so badly about your company to remain on the team. You pay very well and have wonderful benefits, but they do not appreciate what they have. We are looking for that exact job and will be extremely happy if you make room for us on your team.

What exactly seems to be the problem? If they are so unhappy, liberate them! Set them free! We want their spot tomorrow. Have you become so cynical about what is out here that you think there is no one left to hire? There are thousands of us just waiting for the chance to help your team become a winner again. We are excited about exactly what you have to offer.

We continually hear about the shortage of good workers, yet you employ the worst kind. You pay those who do not appreciate you, your organization, or the products and services you provide. You attempt to motivate the very people who speak the worst about you. You paint this wonderful image to the public, yet you keep the darkest of attitudes on your team. That paradox is very confusing to those looking in from the outside.

We are excited about the growth potential and learning opportunities your company has to offer. You have more going for you than you probably know, and we are eager to join your team. You settle for underperformance when there are those of us who can take you to that next level. You attempt to teach people who have no desire to learn. You attempt to coach people who have no desire to play. You attempt to lead people who have no desire to follow. We are right here!

Our positive attitude and willingness to learn quickly will help you brighten every day of your life. We are going to scream and dance if we get that job. But you keep those who moan and groan every day. Why do they deserve the job and we do not get a chance? Was it because they were there first? That makes no sense. You do not have to keep them. Let them go. We want to appreciate what your company has to offer.

Every time you do something positive for the team, they complain. The free lunch was horrible. The safety effort is a joke. The classes you arrange and pay for them to learn are a waste of time. The customers you serve are the problem. You even give them expensive turkeys and hams for the holidays, and all they do is complain. Nothing you do will ever reach them, and we are right here!

Help us understand your dilemma! The solution seems so simple and elemental to us. They do not want what they have, and we do. We are waiting for you to realize that there are more of us out here than you ever imagined.

In today's job market, you are at the talent buffet. Whatever you want is out here waiting and wanting you to scoop us up. We feel like we are yelling and screaming, but you cannot hear us. You must be deafened by the negative voices currently on your team. Dehire them. Stifle the complaints. You cannot control their attitude. What we might miss in experience, we will more than make up for with our positive, can-do attitude.

Our positive attitude will improve your morale, increase your productivity, enhance your customer service, and most of all ... blacken your bottom line. We will brighten your day and ease your workload. After all, how much of your precious time do you currently waste with the wrong people on your team? We can make every aspect of your work life better, but alas, we do not think you see us.

What is blocking your view? Is it the filter of the past? Is it the negative infection you have received from those perpetual bad attitudes on your team? How can we let you know we are out here? When are you going to make room for us on your team?

We know it is never easy to let someone go. We know you will feel horrible while you are doing it. Even if they deserve it, you are a human being and should never enjoy firing an employee. We will make you a promise. Every day of your life will be better when you surround yourself with people who enjoy being on your team. You will never regret the tough decision you definitely need to make. We will have your back if you just give us a chance. Go ahead and make that tough call, then call us. We are waiting!

Signed,

Confused[1]

---

[1] John Grubbs, "Dear Hiring Manager We Are Confused!," *My Time to Lead* (blog), April 25, 2016, http://www.johngrubbs.com/blog/BOSVIEW/Dear-Hiring-Manager-We-Are-Confused/.

Chapter 10

<u>Incentives = Retention</u>

There are many different types of incentives, but they're all used for the same purpose: getting and keeping the right people on the bus. Positive incentives are the heart of an organization's retention program. A well-maintained and robust retention program is inspiring, motivating, and necessary for success. Listed below are just a few reasonable incentives that an organization can offer:

- an ethical work environment

- a clear vision and direction

- a safe place to work

- affordable health insurance

- true leaders in positions of authority

- wages based on performance

- vacations based on performance and seniority

- scheduled turnover of the C team

Financial compensation is not the sole reason the A and B teams are loyal; it's that combined with a culture of love, honor, integrity, and commitment to success.

Listed below are just a few side effects of a robust incentive program:

- increased safety

- more-stable attendance

- greater mutual respect

- tactful honesty

- boosted creativity

- unprompted proactivity

- increased productivity

- more-effective teamwork

- increased profits

Some managers in disguise play games with incentives. They believe that they have the upper hand and that the employee has to accept whatever is or isn't offered. This approach is simply not effective. When incentives other than wages are withheld, the only thing left for the employees to work for is a wage, and that is the one thing every organization has, including your competition, who would love to hire one of your trained employees. Employees leave their families, friends, and homes every day to make an honest living and to support their needs, wants, and desires. We are all in charge of ourselves. We work for the incentives that are offered to us only as long as we want to. When we feel we deserve more than our manager in disguise is willing to give, we will consider going somewhere else to get it if that's what it takes for us to feel satisfied with our chosen career and to better justify our decision to leave our families, friends, and homes in the first place. To strengthen an organization's employee-retention program, reasonable compensation and other incentives should be based on individual performance. The executive who is doing his or her job well and has been consistent across the board in his or her evaluations of the team should already know what each employee is worth. This executive should have no desire to play games that ultimately jeopardize the integrity of the retention program.

Some managers in disguise automatically get defensive when anyone asks for a pay increase or a higher starting wage. Their belief is that they will not be bullied into giving a pay raise or any other incentive. More often than not, the employee or potential new hire is not being a bully or playing games. If a team member or potential new hire asks you to provide an incentive, you're either going to give the person what he or she wants, or you're not. There should be no games and no drama. Yes, you might sign the checks, but that only lasts as long as that employee allows you to. Employees all have the right to have another organization sign their checks. It's your choice to be fair or unfair. I suggest you be fair. If you build a great community, fewer people will quit over money. A true leader doesn't let pride get in the way of the decision-making process. True leaders know their teams are watching. Being humble is a great asset. Without it, arrogance fills the void, and arrogance has no place at any level in an organization.

Telling your team "It's not in the budget" is not a good idea when there are members of the C team still on the bus absorbing some of that budget. Once the C team has been identified, it's time to move them out. Throwing good money toward underperforming employees is just not good business. Your organization's team members need the proper tools to do their work. By freeing up those earnings and incentives that were going to the underperforming, you now have more financial and personal capital to meet value-adding expectations.

Chapter 11

<u>Performance and Seniority</u>

I worked for a company that was, and still is, strictly *seniority based* when it came to employee advancement. No matter the quality of effort nor the passion for the work, the employees still couldn't earn their way to the front of the line to receive the next promotion, pay raise, or any other incentive you can think of, simply because someone else had been working there longer. No matter how many teammates went into the manager's office and went to bat for one another, they still couldn't get past the manager in disguise. Systems like this put an improper emphasis on seniority. Seniority has its place, but it should never affect the success of the mission. Seniority cannot be your sole employee-retention program. An employee's seniority should be used when there is a virtual dead heat regarding merit in a promotion decision, when it's time to schedule vacation a year in advance, or when scheduling days off.

When performance is the basis for your employee-retention program, the bottom line is directly affected in a positive way. Employees tend to unlock the power they have and use it for you, in hopes you will harness it ethically. They will continue to do so as long as they feel the organization's vision for the future is clear and challenging and will lead them to even more successful times. When the employees feel that the quality of their efforts is being continuously recognized, even from the executives at the top, they automatically feel better about their work. This is when all the charts and graphs start heading in the right direction. Once executives recognize that they are only as powerful as their teams allow them to be, they will bear great success. You can have all the authority you want, but it's the team's power that makes it all work.

Chapter 12

Set Up to Fail

I had a great engineer come to me and ask, "Where did I go wrong?" He then told me about all the hard work he'd put into verifying the soundness of his idea. I had been paying close attention to the project and its progress from early on. I had even approached my manager while the project was still in its fairly early stages and expressed my concern that it was never going to work because the wrong people (C team) were on the bus. The real problem was the manager already knew this part of the department was going to be involved in this continuous-improvement project but didn't plan on correcting the team dynamics. His refusal to do anything about this directly affected the outcome of the project. My little piece of insight and concern never made it from my manager to the engineer. Of course, if the manager in disguise as a leader would have fulfilled his duties as he expected everyone else to do and had gotten rid of the C team and put in A or B team members or even a combination of the two, we wouldn't have been in this predicament in the first place. In my view, the manager in disguise had set the engineer up to fail from the start.

Once I realized the manager wasn't about to reveal his incompetence by doing his job, I took action and offered the engineer a solution to his problem. I didn't care so much about being right in my manager's eyes in this instance; I cared about being right for the whole of the company by meeting the engineer's expectations. I had a solution to his problem, and he had a rightful expectation for me to hand it over with a sense of urgency, so I did. I asked him if he could arrange it so a different team could operate the production cell using his new solutions, and he said he could. He arranged it that night. The next morning there were three different teammates and myself in the cell with the original four members of the C team looking at us … and they knew what was about to go down. Of course their immediate perception was that we were trying to make them look bad. We were not after their jobs; we were just being the people we'd said we were going to be when we'd been hired on. Turns out, the engineer was right all along. That day, in that production cell, great things happened. With our creativity, proactivity, passion for our work, and teamwork, we destroyed the previous eight-hour scrap and production records easily while the C team went to another part of the same department and successfully managed to bring down productivity and morale. The production issue followed them while we made the process work for us instead of us work for the process. Finding out that the C team's existence was the root cause of the production-cell problem helped expose many more deficiencies in the company.

In this scenario, there was a lack of a quality effort all the way to the top executives. Rome wasn't built in a day, and you don't engineer and remodel an entire department overnight. There were many meetings with employees at all levels. If you work for a company that is 90 percent reactive and only 10 percent proactive, be prepared for a constant struggle. This approach signifies a culture of laziness on many different levels.

A need for accountability at all levels in this company was in order but never came because of seniority and only the minimum production ever being met. This environment was unfortunate for the hundreds of other employees who were affected by the lack of leadership. Word got out (as it always does) about the events that had transpired, and understandably the A and B teams were completely unmotivated after hearing from their managers in disguise that there was nothing the organization could do about the C team members because they were meeting the minimum requirements. The organization's failure to seize all the other opportunities to discipline the C team, including this one, was just not understandable. The A and B teams expected and felt they deserved better than they got. Some managers in disguise would say to those hundreds of good employees, "Just pay attention to yourselves, and don't worry about the others," as if they were going to do something about the issues. Most of the time, they had no plans to do anything; they were just trying to settle everything down and cover up the crisis before it affected their image or their bosses found out about it. This is why managers in disguise should not have authority.

The bottom line is without a team that is working together, there will always be unnecessary struggles. Please don't get me wrong; when there are choices to make and opportunities to seize, there will always be struggles along the way. It's the unnecessary ones we can and should avoid. These constant unnecessary struggles will continue to hinder progress until they're addressed. One of the main focuses of every company should be to have only the right people on the bus with no exceptions. A lack of a quality effort is unacceptable and must be addressed immediately. True leaders can make these connections all day long, every day; they just need the authority to do something about it.

I submit to you another example showing that being at the top of the organizational chart doesn't automatically mean you're in the right seat. I once had the pleasure of meeting a secretary who was passionate about her job and was a tremendous resource when her teammates needed some assistance. Her direct supervisor was an ethical and organized man who was an inspiration to work for. Her work was fulfilling to her, and the team could see it. The supervisor retired, and chaos took his place. After about one month, I was sure the secretary wasn't inspired anymore. I approached her and mentioned that I had noticed a change in her attitude and performance. I asked if there was anything I could do to be a part of the solution. She asked me to find out who her new supervisor was. "What do you mean?" I asked. She explained that she was frustrated and at the end of her rope because she did not know who her boss was. She said it was a free-for-all with the executives. Everyone was pulling her in different directions, and the lack of communication, organization, and leadership was sapping the motivation right out of her. This roadblock turned out to be impassable for even me.

This once-valuable asset to the organization was driven to her breaking point over the next five months. She made a bad decision, a choice that she normally wouldn't have ever made. She sent an e-mail to the person who she felt was most likely her boss and told him about her transition from a highly motivated and proactive team player to the unmotivated person she had become. This "nastygram" didn't sit very well with this C team executive. Instead of inquiring about how he could be a part of the solution or asking himself about his role in her transformation, he took the easy way out and terminated her employment. This supervisor's and the other executives' arrogance are now being put to bad use on a new, unsuspecting secretary. The rest of the team has noticed the incompetence, arrogance, and unwillingness to put forth a quality effort of multiple executives. However, that's all that's happened; it has only been noticed. When members of the C team are at the top, the A and B teams can't achieve much success due to the lack of direction from the top. This level of incompetence is the cause of the company's high turnover rate and dissatisfied employees. However, rest assured that the C team executives are getting full credit for their efforts.

As a leader, you can avoid setting others up for failure by following these four steps:

1. Start by using the 80-20 rule. Spend 80 percent of your time with your teammates, getting to know them and what they're truly passionate about and capable of, and 20 percent of your time doing value-adding office work.

2. Build relationships with those whom you're trying to lead by finding out what their expectations are of you and delivering on them.

3. Invest time in training your team members well enough that they're not dependent on you.

4. Teach the right members of your team how to perform your duties as well as you can. This will keep operations running smoothly in your absence.

To the manager in disguise, these four steps might appear to be planned obsolescence. True leaders, though, understand that the person who follows these steps will always have influence and a level of success that will solidify his or her positions in the organization.

Chapter 13

The Transition

When a leader is trying to be effective but team members do not view him or her as an effective leader, the process of changing this perception can be brutal. For example, a new executive or manager hired externally has a tough uphill climb ahead because there's bound to be some disgruntled employees who believe the position should have been awarded to them. Teams cannot be handed over to just anyone. The A and B teams will automatically unlock their power and potential for someone new until that someone proves through his or her actions that he or she is not worthy of the teams' power and potential. On the other hand, some members of the C team won't support anyone being promoted unless it's them. The A and B teams give their power to the person that they trust, with the expectation that their power will be used for the good of all. Transitions of leadership take some time, so be patient. Transitioning from someone who was fine with the status quo to a wannabe great leader is an especially monumental task but is an admirable undertaking and one to be proud of. So if you are a wannabe great leader who has just been put in a position of authority, be ready for anything. Some people will make up clever names for you and put up all kinds of roadblocks in an effort to hide their shortcomings and lack of desire to help you or anyone else meet their personal goals. The A and B teams will support your efforts in achieving your goals. Keep up the good fight because eventually you will have the opportunity to meet the A and B teams' expectations and prove to them that you really are the resource they have been looking for.

Five Pieces of Advice for Aspiring Leaders

1) When you ask someone a question, avoid doing it in passing. If you don't have time to listen, don't ask. You should make time to ask questions; this is how you know exactly what your team members expect and what's going on in their lives.

2) The art of caring leadership is exactly what it sounds like. When you love what you do and those you work with, your odds of being great at it grow exponentially. Be compassionate and caring.

3) Whenever you get feedback, be in the moment, be prepared to listen, and understand completely what the other person is trying to relay to you. Leave nothing to interpretation. Ask to hear the feedback again and take notes if you have to. Everyone feels better about themselves when they feel that they're cared for and needed. In the world of business, the more value anyone

can add to the process, the more they're needed. Input is value.

4) To be a successful leader, you must be constantly seen and heard. You must be available. You must be in touch and have your finger on the pulse of the organization.

5) Your team members expect you to provide them with a safe and healthful place to work, use the best hiring strategies in order to hire only the best individuals, distribute the workload evenly, offer incentives to advance, and allow room for advancement. These things won't happen all by themselves and cannot be done by sitting behind a desk with your feet propped up and the radio on.

The authority you possess will not make the organization successful by itself. You ultimately need the power the team has, combined with the fragile authority you have, if you're going to be successful. Your authority is fragile because it is directly tied to the organization's success. For example, let's say the production expectation is one hundred pieces an hour, and the team members, for whatever reason, are holding back their power and potential. Chances are you will get one hundred pieces an hour and not one more piece. On the other hand, if the team believes in you and trusts you will do great things with their power, then you might get considerably more production from the team than the bare minimum required to keep their jobs. If you think about it, government shutdowns and behavioral production shutdowns are both products of dysfunction and incompetence within positions of authority. Such shutdowns are usually due to a lack of respect between the managers in disguise and the teams that they lead. On the other hand, when people in positions of authority see that expectations are a two-way street and consistently exceed their team members' expectations, their teams will be inspired to do the same.

Chapter 14

<u>Steps to Success</u>

1. Take accountability for your own actions.

2. Meet your own expectations.

3. Lead by example with discipline at all times.

4. Don't point the finger and deflect the issues that are slowing down success. Instead take accountability for your actions and proactively take action to be a part of the solution.

5. Treat everyone as your customer. Find out what their expectations are, and deliver on those expectations in a timely manner.

6. Keep your proverbial in-box empty. Try not to get behind, and proactively meet or exceed the requirements of your work. Somewhere somebody is waiting for what's in your in-box. Expectations are in your in-box.

7. Be the resource everyone wants to be in touch with. If you're the last person your team comes to for knowledge or assistance, you're probably in the wrong seat on the bus. You should move to the right seat and let another wannabe great leader have a shot at it.

8. Know your limitations and be the best at knowing when to say no. If you get in over your head because you can't say no, then you run the risk of not having the capacity to successfully exceed your customers' expectations. This is unacceptable.

9. Perform a regularly scheduled cost-benefit analysis on the C team members. This will assist you in determining the indirect cost for subsidizing poor performers and better help the organization as a whole with future resource allocations that add value.

10. Never let members of the C team train their replacements. Stop the cycle.

11. Never promote someone to his or her level of incompetence. Just because there's an open position doesn't mean it should be filled with just anybody. Putting some thought into the promotion process will keep you from setting someone up for failure or embarrassment. Setting them up for failure in this way is bad for them, and it's bad for everyone on the bus. Some people could be driven to make unethical decisions they usually would not make if put into this situation.

Chapter 15

<u>Overcoming the Roadblocks to Success</u>

Roadblock: The manager who doesn't want to do the real work of leading

I get fired up when a manager in disguise tells me to come back to the real world or says I'm dreaming about the impossible in an attempt to slow me down. All the while he or she is steadily sweeping issues under the carpet to hide his or her incompetence and lack of passion.

Solution: Lead him or her by example. Proactively exceed everyone's expectations better than anyone else. Build the influence the manager only wishes he or she had.

Roadblock: Corrupt data

Imagine the engineer who's trying to make the process better with corrupt data from a manager in disguise. Sweeping expectations and issues under the carpet affects everyone from the top executive to the newest teammate. Greatness is possible! All it takes is people seizing opportunities, making well-thought-out choices, and being disciplined. This culture of thought will make the process work for you instead of you working for the process.

Solution: Make certain that only the right people are on the bus. It's the people who don't belong on the bus who feel the need to alter data to make themselves look better than they really are.

Roadblock: People taking credit for everyone else's efforts

Inevitably you're going to run into those who will try to slow down your efforts and your success and who will take credit for everyone else's efforts in a pathetic attempt to make themselves look good.

Solution: Once again, make certain that only the right people are on the bus. This will eliminate those who feel they have to take credit for the quality of someone else's efforts to make themselves stand out.

Roadblock: Goals that are set so high even the A team members can't reach them

Inevitably you're going to run into managers in disguise who arbitrarily set goals so high they are impossible to meet. These managers in disguise do this in an attempt to make themselves look good for trying while everyone else looks bad for not succeeding. Pay close attention to the off shifts in regard to this tactic. It's easy for people to take credit for something they didn't do when there's nobody around to keep them honest.

Don't worry too much about these types, though; the team is comparing them to you, and if you're leading by example with consistent great discipline, these managers in disguise will be recognized for who they really are. Lack of results will be their downfall.

Solution: Always build up your team. Evaluate goals as they are set and ensure they are reasonable and achievable. Instead of allowing a manager in disguise to create lose-lose situations by imposing unrealistic goals, how about advising him or her to set realistic goals and create a win-win situation? Most people in all organizations respect a challenge when one comes along; it breaks up the day-to-day monotony. Setting goals that are so aggressive that no one can succeed breaks the team's morale. Everyone likes the taste of victory every once in a while, so set goals that are challenging but not impossible. The positive atmosphere gained is worth more to the organization than a demoralized team that has suffered yet another loss.

Roadblock: The manager who feels threatened by those who exceed expectations

Don't forget about the manager in disguise who sees you exceeding expectations on many different levels and feels they have to remind you who's in charge. In his or her infinite wisdom, this manager may decide to call you to his or her office, always doing so in front of the whole team to make a scene. He or she will sit you down in the tiny chair in front of his or her desk for a chat in which they attempt to convince you just how hard his or her position is. I've always found this approach amusing. This has happened to me several times. Each time I said, "I'm impressed, just not favorably." Nothing says "I'm in charge" more than sitting behind a desk. Here is why his or her position is hard: Odds are he or she has been caught asking the team to deliver on his or her expectations when he or she is not willing to do the same for the team in return. Odds are he or she is managing all personalities the same and expecting them to all respond the same. And odds are he or she lacks passion for the work and has a reactive mentality, which invites endless issues. It shouldn't take a bribe or hypnosis to get someone to do his or her job. If it does, then that person is obviously in the wrong seat. If you're truly passionate about leadership, taking it to the next level is easy and rewarding.

Solution: Keep making great choices and seizing all opportunities. Separate yourself from your competition in a positive manner. The manager has the same opportunities as you do; make the manager work to keep his or her job. Your teammates will love you for your proactivity.

Roadblock: Superficial meetings

Meetings are necessary, but more often than not, they become roadblocks. Some meetings turn into amateur hour and become a waste of time, resources, and money. For instance, let's say there's a personality conflict between a team and its manager in disguise that needs to be addressed immediately. The failing manager's boss gathers everyone involved in a meeting to discuss the issue. The failing manager is placed in the front of the room, and his boss asks everyone to discuss the issue at hand. To no one's surprise, you could hear a pin drop. No value is being added here, and this is by design. The boss hired the manager and promoted him to his level of incompetence, and the boss wants this issue to just go away. So the boss makes it look as if he gave it his best shot by conducting a meeting. Of course the team has nothing to say. Nobody's going to tell the boss how he or she really feels in that situation due to fear of retaliation, and the boss knows it. So the meeting ends, and the cycle continues. This type of meeting is very effective if your goal is to stifle progress. What this boss isn't taking into account is the massive indirect cost of not addressing the issue before him. Unfortunately, many organizations never apply a cost-benefit analysis to the C team members. Most organizations don't even realize that this step is a requirement for organizational and personal success.

Another non-value-adding meeting is the superficial meeting about how to increase efficiency, quality, and profits and reduce waste. This one is the most expensive of all the superficial meetings. The executives and managers get together and brainstorm ideas about how to make what they have better. During this meeting, not once will anyone ask, "Before we get started with anything else, do we have only the right people on the bus?" The right people are the most important issue here. Not having the right people is probably why this meeting is being held in the first place. The ideas that come from this type of meeting are useless. Without the right people on the bus in the first place, you're just spinning your wheels.

Solution: Make certain that only the right people are on the bus. Once again, having the wrong people on the bus is a lose-lose situation for the entire organization. Failure to turn over the C team on a regular basis is very costly to management's credibility. If team members don't trust that management is taking their work seriously, it can seriously affect how they react to what management has to say.

Roadblock: Wrongly identified go-to people

In every organization there are subject matter experts (SMEs). These are supposed to be the go-to people. However, many organizations will put just about anyone on the SME list just to make the person feel good. This takes all credibility out of the program. Without credibility, the list becomes useless. If you're the last person the team would come to for guidance, you shouldn't be on the list. A robust SME list, complete with ethical and respectable people, can truly get your charts and graphs headed in the right direction.

Solution: Build a list of people who you think your teammates would agree fit the acceptance criteria for an SME list. Prior to implementing the list, offer it to all who could benefit from it for their approval. To get the most out of the SME list, revisit the list on a regular schedule.

Chapter 16

<u>Terminations</u>

When you terminate someone's employment, it means you are no longer in need of their services. When an employee quits, it means they're no longer in need of your services, effectively terminating you. An employee quitting should always be thoroughly investigated. Why do good employees quit? They quit when

- their expectations haven't been met for extended periods of time,

- the organization is headed in the wrong direction,

- management won't remove managers in disguise to allow true leaders into these positions,

- they don't feel recognized,

- their jobs aren't fun anymore,

- they've become the problem (the wrong person on the bus).

All these issues stem from a lack of effective leadership. Even good employees have their limits as to the amount of dysfunction they can take. Once a person's morale is beaten into submission, he or she usually seeks other opportunities to make a difference elsewhere and then quit. Once a good employee recognizes the organization is led by C team executives, he or she will start to figure out just how far down the organizational chart the corruption goes. With this information he or she can see how much room for advancement there is and will begin to start making decisions about his or her future. If there is light at the end of the tunnel, the employee will stay. If the employee feels there is no hope left for advancement because the light at the end of the tunnel has been turned off until new leadership arrives, the employee will begin implementing his or her exit strategy. A good employee's length of service is directly related to his or her view of the effectiveness of the organization's leadership. A good employee who is frustrated will inevitably become less and less passionate about elevating the organization. A good employee will quit before he or she begins to destroy the motivation of others. (This type of sacrifice is only made by good employees.) If a good employee is thinking about quitting, leadership should always find out why and do something about it. After all, that's what incentives are for, to entice the right people into getting on the bus in the first place and to keep them there.

When it comes to employees that should be terminated, all too often managers in disguise are unable to deliver, no matter how much trouble the person is, because of pure laziness or cowardice. They will deflect and say something like "I'm working on the issue" or "Everyone needs a job, and this stuff takes time." This lack of a quality effort in resolving the issues stemming from the C team is only the case until it's time to cut costs and overhead or the substandard employee in question finally affects the manager directly. Then the free ride is over faster than you can say "You're fired." This mentality is nonsense.

Over the course of several years, I have crossed paths with some managers in disguise who didn't have a clue what it means to be a leader, but no one could convince them of it. No discussions, examples, or even number one best-selling authors of leadership material could make these guys consider a different leadership approach from the one they'd taught themselves. Of course, these guys had been hired directly through the buddy system. I would quote something from a very successful leadership author or well-known leadership guru, and these guys would automatically deflect, generalize, and argue that their way was better. Needless to say, I couldn't waste too much of my time on these types. I had the solution to the problem, which was to find a different seat for them on the bus if there was one and replace them with the first A player I could find. I just didn't have the authority to implement the solution. The bosses/best friends of these miserably failing managers were the ones with the authority, but they didn't have the desire to do the right thing for the greater good. You can come up with your own conclusions about the culture of these organizations and the level of incompetence that the C team executives were willing to tolerate. This is just another example of why good employees leave.

When a good employee quits, an exit interview and an in-house investigation are warranted. This is the perfect time to reevaluate who's on the bus, whether they are all in the right seats, who needs to get off the bus, and how close you are to losing more of your A and B team members. Don't delay. The organization and team deserve expediency in addressing any potential issues that are identified.

When it comes to a termination, the former employee is either going to be a member of your outside sales force or not. The outcome mostly hinges on the culture of the organization. An employee who feels that he or she was treated with respect and that the organization always put its values before profits could get on his or her social media accounts and reach thousands of people in a short period of time. On the other hand, an employee who feels just the opposite because the organization was led by C team executives could get on his or her social media accounts and attempt to destroy everything the organization is trying to accomplish. Employees fire themselves every day; they know when their time is up. It's up to the leaders to seize these unfortunate opportunities and do their best to add value to the team by replacing the former employees with A or B team members. Doing this will reassure team members that the leaders are really looking out for the team's best interests. Replacing a member of the C team with a member of the A or B teams communicates to the team that you have heard their expectations, that you are delivering on those expectations, and that there is no better place to work. If a leader has performed his or her job to the best of his or her ability and the employees know and understand this, then the leader has increased his or her odds for success. Terminations have a greater effect on smaller businesses. Prior to terminating anyone's employment, leadership should make every effort to ensure that the organization has fulfilled its duty to make the employees happy and successful. Attempting to meet or exceed the organization's, employees', and customers' expectations can be a lot of work, but the reward for meeting or exceeding those expectations in a timely manner is well worth it.

Years ago I was working two jobs. My main job was in a manufacturing facility, and my side job was at a vehicle-accessories shop where we built custom trucks. Everyone in the shop thought of each other as leaders, and we only hired the best. There were some C team members who slipped through in our hiring process, but they didn't last long. They must have thought we were kidding when we said our team was going to be reporting back on a daily basis about whether or not they were a great fit for us. There were only twelve of us, and we were very efficient. We were one big happy family. Everyone was inspired, empowered, and in charge. If the team was dissatisfied with the quality of someone's effort, we discussed it; we put forth a quality effort to ensure we were exceeding the expectations of the person in question. Everyone answered to everyone, and it was awesome. Then it happened. One of our teammates made a very bad choice that required his termination. A customer brought the issue to our attention, and we addressed it immediately as a team. Our dear friend and teammate owned up to the error in judgment quickly and apologized to us like a man. He offered no excuses. He knew from his years of working with us that the policies were going to be enforced without exceptions, and he also knew his termination was of his own doing. Never once did he have anything bad to say about any of us. He loved us as we loved him. This experience brought our team even closer. He later went to work for a local car dealership and told them about our way of conducting ourselves and our business and how our solutions could even add value to the car dealership. Some would call this work environment an anomaly or say it was only possible because we had a small team. These people have yet to see the big picture and may never. Many organizations, due to their love and passion for their work, have built great working environments, which have been written about in many books. When it comes to facilitating the building of a great community inside your organization, size doesn't matter. It's the implementation of conscious choices and discipline that most people desire to be a part of.

Chapter 17

<u>Hiring</u>

Hiring people can be very profitable and rewarding. With a well-thought-out, well-rehearsed hiring strategy and a passion for meeting the team's/organization's expectations, forward progress, due to organizational satisfaction, can be found in all aspects of every organization. It's my belief that people should be hired based on their passion for the open position, their potential, and their confidence in their abilities as opposed to a college degree or current competency in the work expected. New skills can be taught; the added value is in a person's passion, potential, and confidence.

Usually, the first temptation in hiring is to hire someone you know. The perception of a sure thing is attractive. If the people doing the hiring have college degrees, then it's likely that their friends and people they know will have one as well. Some organizations will make a college degree a requirement for certain positions in order to prevent current employees without college degrees from seeking promotions into those positions. By disqualifying these employees, the managers in disguise can hire who they want, a.k.a. people they already know. This strategy totally demoralizes senior members of the A team. These passionate, hardworking team players who have been employing the bottom-up style of leadership, in an attempt to help keep the bus moving in the right direction, are the ones who deserve a shot at promotions, with or without a college degree.

I've listed below a few questions you should ask yourself when you're the one charged with the task of hiring the best. These questions give an alternative to the status quo of the hiring process. This hiring strategy is my attempt to give some common sense to those who don't have any and to make the not so obvious, obvious.

1. What does your team expect of you? They expect you to use the best hiring strategy in order to hire the best employees. No hiring strategies are foolproof, but you can increase your odds of hiring the right people whom the team will accept if you put forth the effort to only hire the best. The team will be exposed to the quality of your effort, and through their actions and responses they will let you know if you're meeting their expectations or not. Remember, profits drop when expectations aren't met. How far are you willing to go before you decide to get with the program?

2. Have you fully explained to the candidate what the team's expectations are? You should be in constant contact with your team members in order to find out their specific expectations. Explain to the candidate that

you are expected to hire only the best people who will not ask the team to pull their weight. You should tell potential hires just how fast they're going to be off the bus if they end up not being who they say they are in their interviews, because your team deserves better. This tactic is designed to keep the interviewee honest, because if the interviewee is not honest, he or she will be looking for another job real soon. This is not a scare tactic; this is love for the team. The potential hire can and will expect the same level of love, respect, and commitment from you if he or she is hired. No surprises here: explaining the culture up front is a great way to start.

3. How does the candidate's dream job relate (or not relate) to this job? Ask the candidate about his or her dream job. If it has nothing to do with the organization's destination, then he or she is not right for the team. Don't waste everybody's time and your profits. Remember, however, that the candidate's dream and the company's destination may not be about what the company is doing but *how* they are doing it. Many great employees had no previous knowledge of a company's workings, but the company gave them the environment for success.

4. Have you explained in detail to the prospective employee what the position would look like on a day where everything that could go wrong actually does go wrong? By the time you get to this step, the potential hire is either sure of himself or herself or second-guessing

himself or herself. Only the interviewees know if they're being completely honest and setting themselves and everyone else up for failure or if they're inspired by the opportunity to work with your organization. This step is designed to solidify the potential hire's position on the matter. As the explanation of the job unfolds, your job is to read into the interviewee's actions and responses to what you're telling him or her. You don't need someone who appears to be desperate and has no other options. You need someone with ideas, passion, and confidence.

Conclusion

What is the meaning behind the title *Managers in Disguise—Leaders in Disgust*? It is simple! Leaders shouldn't be distracted by having to do other people's jobs and tasks. Genuine leaders have key qualities that make them special. They are able to recognize employees' unique strengths and weaknesses and utilize them to optimize and improve the organization as a whole. They want to make the most of every opportunity by elevating other leaders to positions where they can positively influence others. There is no place for arrogance and pride in positions of leadership. Listening to disgruntled employees and addressing their concerns is important. Employees and values are more important than profits, and as long as employees and values are nurtured, profits will come naturally. At the same time, companies should be fair and just in their compensation, which should be based on merit, not simply longevity. Companies must give employees the tools needed to do the job right while holding everyone to the same standard of accountability. Leaders can only be made from those willing to be leaders, and leaders must understand that others' expectations of them will be higher once they assume positions of authority. Always remember, roadblocks are inevitable, but with genuine leadership, they are never impossible to overcome.

For a quick verification of your understanding of the principles this book addresses, visit www.leadersindisgust.com and download the short quiz.

Also consider the following questions:

1. Have you ever worked for a manager in disguise? How did it affect your work? Did you look forward to coming to work every day?

2. Have you ever worked for a true leader? What did you learn from that experience?

3. What do you think are the most important qualities of a leader?

4. If you were in a position of authority, what would you do to ensure effective leadership throughout your organization?

5. What questions would you ask a potential new hire in a job interview?

Printed in the United States
By Bookmasters